C000186627

MARKING MILESTONES

Irene Howat

All rights reserved

No part of this publication may be reproduced,
stored in a retrieval system, or transmitted in
any form by any means, electronic, mechanical,
photocopying, recording or otherwise, without the
prior permission of The Handsel Press Ltd

British Library Cataloguing in Publication Data:
a catalogue record for this publication
is available from the British Library

ISBN   978-1-912052-71-4

© Handsel Press

The right of Irene Howat to be identified as the
author of this work has been asserted by her in
accordance with the Copyright, Designs and Patents
Act 1988

Typeset in 12pt Minion Pro at Haddington, Scotland

Printed by West Port Print, St Andrews

Contents

MARKING MILESTONES

A collection of poems –
a little bit of myself
for
my grandchildren
Euan and Eilidh, Rowan and Magnus

Jack Frost

Ice etched fern fronds
chip the sunrise
on my early morning window
breathing cold radiance
on the start of my day.

And all that is left
by coffee time?
Some condensation
on the window sill
and the memory of beauty
that only happens once
and only needs to.

For which of us
who met Jack Frost
childhood years ago
would fail to recognise him
once again?

Regimental Tulips

regimental tulips
stand to attention
guarding the honour
of spring

daffodils
can hardly blow their trumpets
for cavorting in the wind
skirts barely decent

on-duty tulips
don't stand easy
till retirement
when
weary of parade
they relax in blowsy shamelessness

but the daffodils
are not there to see them
they died .   .   .
laughing

The Pianist

Slim fingers
dance on ivory.

Earth's rock heart
melts and swells ripe plum-like,
bursts and spills itself,
heaving to the very edge of pain
and back.

Staccatos rocket high
and land
to spring and tumble.
Melodies trickling into cracks
wait eagerly
for catch-me-if-you-can.

Slim fingers
beat a pulse,
and I can breathe again.

The Sea

The sea
is a zillion diamonds
treasure chested
in rock and sand
bursting at the seams
to spill itself out
and dress
the whole earth
for a party.

The Last Day

Buttoned into the shoreside
the cottage sat, staring
through gingham eyes
as forever ceased to be.

Forever the sea had marked the beat
on the black rock,
forever the wind had combed
clean through the marram grass.

Then the gable cracked
and the cottage was no more.

And there was morning
and there was evening
the last day.

The Rowan Tree

Clinging to the rock face
she wedges in a crevice
to shelter from the storm,
pitting her frailty
against everything winter throws at her.

When the worst is past
she stretches tentatively,
easing thread roots along an outcrop,
willing them into cracks too fine to see,
snow-melt and tenacity keeping her alive.

Her first unfurled leaves
testify to the impossible.

Meconopsis

Dry blocks in my paint box
challenge me:
Cerulean blue, New Gamboge
and Alizarin Crimson,
names that make me tingle
with anticipation.

Will they give themselves
to the happy accidents
water-colourists dream of?
Will they flow into,
        grow into *Meconopsis*,
the Himalayan blue poppies
that bloom in my mind's eye?

A Winter's Tale

Evening was Nan's time of day.
On summer evenings,
work done, chores finished,
she took herself into her garden
where she planted and potted,
weeded and pruned
to her heart's content.

Winter evenings were different.
On winter evenings
Nan settled beside the fire,
surrounded, near engulfed,
by squares of cloth each waiting
to find its final resting place
in one of her patchwork quilts.
There she placed and pinned,
tacked and stitched
to her heart's content.

As Nan sewed floral patches she thought
of those who deserved bouquets –
all who helped and cared,
nurtured and served.
Bright patterns reminded her of young folk
and she patched in her hopes for them.
Those who labour were remembered
when busily patterned fabrics found their places.
Sombre squares made her think of powerful people.

Stitch by stitch she wished for them
wisdom and integrity.
Old and faded fabrics brought
old and faded faces
and she prayed for their contentment.

Stitch by stitch and hour by hour,
square by square and winter by winter,
Nan wrapped everyone in patchwork
in her single-handed effort
to keep the whole world warm.

Pebbles

pebbles rumble
as a wave breaks
then settle
preening themselves in the sun
only to be bubble battered
picture shattered
pebble scattered
by a white horse
that canters to the shore
                              to die

Wind-whipped Waves

Wind whipped waves
stampede the shore,
thrashing,
crashing into a trillion chips
of light.

A solitary rock
catapults the sea
back on itself

and shudders

when a slither

t

    r

      i

        c

          k

            l

               e

                  s

t ~~~ i ~~~ c ~~~ k ~~~ l ~~~ e ~~~ s

d o w n   i t s   b a c k.

On the Third Day

On the third day God created autumn.
Plants and trees of the land he made,
by the word of his power, and each
bore seeds or fruits according to their kinds.
So God created autumn.

On the sixth day he looked at all he'd made:
sun and seas, animals and birds,
flowers, clouds, high mountains and mankind,
and all the different seasons of the year.
God saw that every one of them was good.

Plants and trees wore their brightest colours,
to celebrate the future of their kinds –
the autumns of tomorrow.

And then they held their breath,
watching
as fruits lay on fertile ground,
as seeds fell on rich brown soil.

Then dropping their leaves gently as a blanket
they settled their future to sleep.

Resurrection

bracken fires in April dryness
victim of sun and shard of glass

embers of hillside
acrid air
a death-long day's work

charred branches
claw heaven
with their why

rain reduces the hillside to tears
that in their flowing
wash away streaks of ash
freeing a solitary shoot
of Easter green

Thunderstorm

21.03   Three individuals
working individually:
Dad in his study
        poring over papers,
me on the phone,
        as usual,
daughter doing homework.
What's new?

The bang was new,
both crash and flash were new.
Darkness followed,
ancient and empty.

21.05   filled the instant Dad arrived
dark behind his torch,
then daughter with candles
        – cinnamon scented –
and concern.

21.15   for ten minutes
we worked as one:
found the gas lantern,
phoned Scottish Power
and candlelit the house.

21.25   Three individuals
working individually:
Dad in his study
peering at his papers,
me on the phone,
as usual,
daughter doing candlelit,
cinnamon-scented homework.

The Last One Left

It's a strange thing
being the last one left,
the last one left
of a family of three.

For as long as I remember
I had a brother on either side.
Now there is no-one,
there is no-one
to check out my memories.

Did Dad actually say that?
Did Mum really make a pudding
called white apple?
Did the three of us
argue as much as I think we did
before the truce,
the truce
that grew into friendship?

I will believe my memories
and pass some of them on.
If I don't,
if I don't
no one will know about white apple.

The First Hymn

The first hymn was
just long enough
for Flora to pull her skirt
until the pleats were where they ought to be.
She'd dressed in a rush.

It took her the whole prayer
to work out
the week's meals.

The intimations allowed Flora
to worry about lunch.
Had she turned down the oven?

The sermon lasted
the total count of all the panes
in both arched windows,
the sum of the top three numbers
on the hymn board
divided by the bottom one,
plus two presbyterian peppermints.

And the benediction?
It hit Flora like a hammer blow -
for the very first time.

She left
a new woman.

Marking a Milestone

The time has come to mark a milestone,
to take note of miles travelled,
looking back over cloudy days
and finding they no longer cast long shadows,
remembering sunny days too,
stopping to feel their warmth
still beating on your back.

The stone has an engraving
of miles still to be travelled
but the sun shines too brightly
to read it.

The time has come to face the sun full on,
casting your shadow on the past
and not the future.

You will know when you reach home
for God's Son will be the sun
and the warmth will be his warmth
of welcome.

Tuesday Drawer

Where would I be without my cleaner?
She makes up for my deficiencies
as a housewife,
working wonders
while we go for a walk each Tuesday.

We always go out
for fear of being sucked
into the vacuum cleaner
or buffed to a shine.

She's impressed by my tidy study
and often says so.
I smile …
and think of my Tuesday drawer.

It lies empty six days a week.
On the seventh I sweep everything
off my desk, my table and the floor
into my Tuesday drawer
only to take it out again
when we return from our walk.

Don't tell her.

If I Had a Cow

Aunt Bella was a widow
with two children to bring up
and a croft to work.

She had some cows, hens
– there was always one called Geggly –
and two or three fields
where she over-wintered ewes.

The cows all had names.
There was Mabel and Maud
in neighbouring stalls,
and Maggie and Ella
in the next ones down.

They were called after far-out cousins
she liked to remember,
folk she wanted her children
to know were family.

If I had a cow,
I'd call her Bella.

Summer Dress

When I was eight my summer dress
had a Peter Pan collar, puffed sleeves
and a skirt wide enough to twirl in.
The top was smocked
and the belt tied in a bow at the back.
It was a fine dress.
It was brown.

Winter is brown, a brown wraparound blanket.

Spring is brown polkadotted with green,
snowdrop white and crocus purple.

Autumn is brown swirled with gold
all rumpled and crumpled together
with red, orange, yellow and green.

Summer is sunshine splashed with marigolds,
delphinium stripes speckled with forget-me-nots,
bold poppy red clashing shamelessly
with every colour of lupin
and tiny specks of meadowsweet twinkling like stars,
all against a background of sand gold and sea green.

Yes, it was a fine dress,
but not, I think, a summer dress
for an eight-year-old.

Parting from Nancy

I did not know
the last time we kissed
was the very last time
and I am glad.

We parted lightly
expecting
a little more time together.
Had we known
we might have said
too much.

Words
make heavy memories.

Our kiss was light
as the touch
of a butterfly.
I still feel it.

The Cherry Tree

You stand
stark
accusing the wind
of unbuttoning your autumn outfit
and blowing
your coat of many colours
away.

Away
below the beech hedge
      to blanket crocus blubs
      against winter's fury.

Away
behind the garden shed
      swirling a cocoon
      around a hedgehog.

Branches akimbo
you confront the wind,
calling it
uncaring.

The Echo

The sun's midsummer rays
lower in the Finnish sky
as I sit outside a church
in Espoo.

Silence falls when the organ sounds,
quietly at first
and then swelling,
filling the church
and the midnight world.

Then the deepest voice I have ever heard
strikes the lowest note
as Nicolai Gedda wrenches at my heart.

Utterly steadily,
painfully purely,
the men of Uspenskin
join in so quietly
that I lean forward
to hear.

I breathe the music rather than hear it;
the harmonics are exquisite.

When the last note fades
I strain to catch
the heartbeat of the choir
and cling to the echo

    of the echo

        of the echo . . .

Heritage

Backs sore thinning row upon row
of turnips,
and hacking seam after seam
of unforgiving coal.

Hands raw scrabbling through tunnels
in the dark,
canary singing,
and easing leeks from winter's grip.

Fingers scratched by calves' rough tongues
in a milk bucket
and by a wire nailbrush
that never scraped away coal dust.

Wearied by hard labour
in field or pit
folk crept to bed
and slept
till halfway through the night
when their day began.

I was hewn from the coal seams
and rocky soil of Ayrshire,
and sometimes I don't sleep well.

The Sea at Machrihanish

It's hardly a splashing
this sound of swell
that has moulded my breathing
to its rhythm.

From time to time a wave
breaks over a rock and then,
recognising its offence,
slides guiltily
down the landward side.

Thrift and bladder campion
are buttoned between the rocks,
the rocks that are as they always have been.
Lichen pins them to the past.

The Spider

All night long she wove
a web of finest silk,
hanging it out on a bush to dry

and try
to catch for breakfast
some insect
all unsuspecting
on its early morning flight

but caught instead
a million drops of sunlight.

Sunrise over Arran

the sun's fingers
stroke
Arran awake.

stretching her hills
into the morning
she eases off
her cloud pyjamas

puzzles for a while
what to wear

then dresses
in a floral print

Reflections

The wind sighs
through the tree tops.
Leaves and little branches
respond to her caress
and settle
in the still
of the night.

Pinpoints of starlight
search for their reflections
and find them
in the early morning dew.

Thank You, My Friend

Thank you for green time
fresh and full of promise.

Thank you for yellow time
exciting and free.

Thank you for blue time
deep and moving.

Thank you for brown time,
warm earth brown time,
especially for brown time.

Eternity

eternity is
a year and a day
world without end
for ever and ever

the throb of toothache
a kiss
and three o'clock in the morning
of a sleepless night

eternity is
the lifetime of a polythene bag
and a plastic rose
for ever and ever
and ever and ever
and ever . . . . .

Dawn

Dawn slides across the sky
and stretches,
reaching out her fingers
of light
to stroke the day awake.

'This is the day,' she beams,
'This is the day God made.'
Her nimble fingers tickle the earth.
'Rejoice,' she says, 'and be glad in it.'

Fizz

'Shhhh ... sit at peace,'
the command was whispered,
'and listen.'

'I've got fizzy feet,'
he whined church-quietly.
Pins and needles mean nothing
at four,
fizz does.

But listen he did
and deep teaching
a child can understand
stilled him.

God's Son Jesus
was a really truly boy -
and he knows
and remembers
what fizzy feet feel like.

Rufus

Rufus hated his name
for the second time today
– and today was a good day.

'Rufus,' barked his father
when he was three.
'Not Roofus, kid.
You're not a dog.'

'Ruefus,' his first teacher
registered each morning.
'Rueful,' she joked,
when he looked crestfallen,
and then forgot it.

Every five year old in the class
sponged up the thought
and 'Roofool' stuck like superglue.

Jenny was different.
She called him Rufus
till she called him Darling.
And today she'd call him Daddy
for the very first time.

'Well, Daddy,' Jenny purred,
handing him their newborn son.

'Are you calling him after yourself?'
asked the midwife.
'No way!' he assured her.
'I hate my name.'
(for the third time today)
'My boy has a name to be proud of.'

'We're calling him Elvis.'
It was Jenny who spoke
for her husband was drowning
in two deep dark eyes.
'You'll like that, son, won't you?'
she ordered gently,
stroking his black spiky hair.

Elvis opened his new mouth wide
and yelled.

Time

time
ticks to-
wards
tomorrow to-
day
tocks a-
way
      the
clock's
hands
chip off
minutes
chop
chew
chomp through
days re-
lentlessly until

e t e r n i t y d r o w n s t h e t y r a n y o f t i m e

a n d

e ... v ... e ... r ... y

  c ... l ... o ... c ... k

    i . . . s

      s . . . t . . i . . l . . . l